Strategic Studies Institute
and
U.S. Army War College Press

A SOLDIER'S MORALITY, RELIGION, AND OUR PROFESSIONAL ETHIC: DOES THE ARMY'S CULTURE FACILITATE INTEGRATION, CHARACTER DEVELOPMENT, AND TRUST IN THE PROFESSION?

Don M. Snider
Alexander P. Shine

April 2014

FOREWORD

This monograph is the 6th in the Professional Military Ethics Series; it addresses an issue about which little has been written. It intentionally plows new and difficult ground.

The larger issue it addresses is the cultures of the military professions which currently serve our Republic and the role of the Stewards of the Profession in the evolution of those cultures, in particular their moral and ethical core. Since our Armed Forces exist as military professions only by the trust they earn from the society they serve and the trust they engender among professionals who voluntarily serve within them, this issue is of no small import. If the Stewards are unable to lead the professions such that both the external and internal trust relationships are maintained, then the military institution reverts to its alternative organizational character of a big, lumbering government bureaucracy. Since there is no historical record that such government bureaucracies are able to create the expert knowledge or expert practice of a modern, military profession—such as we have enjoyed in the post-Vietnam era—such a situation does not bode well for the future security of the Republic.

Thus, the larger issue has to do with the evolution of the ethics of America's military professions. Those ethics, however, do not exist nor evolve in isolation of other influences external to the professions. Scholars have established for some time that there are three major influences on the ethics of the military professions: 1) the changing nature of warfare and the associated imperative to prosecute it effectively; 2) the evolving values of the society being defended [both their beliefs as to what is moral or ethical in warfare, and more broadly what they value as a society]; and, 3) the international treaties and conventions to which the United States is a party. It is the second of these influences that is of interest in this monograph—the evolving values of the American society being defended.

Among the evolving values of American society, this research seeks to address the perennial issue of religion, its role in the moral character of individual volunteers, and how, amid a secularizing society, the Stewards of the Professions can maintain an ethical culture that facilitates, indeed fosters, both correct religious expression and military effectiveness. Since the military represents a microcosm of American society, the cultural wars raging outside the professions for several decades on such issues as racial integration, abortion, the service of gays in the military, gender roles, etc., have each migrated in their own time into the military sub-society. This research explores the extent to which that is now the case with religious expression and how the military professions can, once again, lead in overcoming such cultural dysfunction, in this case by facilitating soldiers' individual integration of diverse personal moralities, faith–based or not, with their profession's ethic.

Since this is an initial effort in this area of research, we expect that it will serve its intended purpose — to start a dialogue within our military professions on this vital and urgent issue.

DOUGLAS C. LOVELACE, JR.
Director
Strategic Studies Institute and
    U.S. Army War College Press

EVERETT DENTON KNAPP, JR.
Colonel, Infantry, U.S. Army
Director
Center for the Army Profession
    and Ethic (CAPE)
Combined Arms Center
    U.S. Army Training and
    Doctrine Command

ABOUT THE AUTHORS

DON M. SNIDER is a Professor Emeritus of Political Science at West Point, NY, from which he retired in 2008. He is now a Senior Fellow in the Center for the Army Profession and Ethic (CAPE) at West Point and an Adjunct Research Professor in the Strategic Studies Institute at the U.S. Army War College, Carlisle, PA. In a previous military career, Dr. Snider served three combat tours in Vietnam as an infantryman; after battalion command, he served as Chief of Plans for Theater Army in Europe, as Joint Planner for the Army Chief of Staff, as Executive Assistant in the Office of the Chairman of the Joint Chiefs of Staff, and on the staff of the National Security Council in the White House. He retired from the Army in 1990. Dr. Snider's research examines American civil-military relations, the identities and development of the American Army officer, military professions, and professional military ethics. He was research director and co-editor of *The Future of the Army Profession*, (2d Ed., New York: McGraw-Hill, 2005), and *Forging the Warrior's Character* (2d Ed., New York: McGraw-Hill, 2008). More recent publications include, "Dissent and Strategic Leadership of Military Professions" (*Orbis*, 2008), *The Army's Professional Military Ethic in an Era of Persistent Conflict* (co-author, Carlisle, PA: Strategic Studies Institute, U.S. Army War College, 2008) and, co-editor with Suzanne Nielsen, *American Civil-Military Relations: The Soldier and the State in the New Era*, (Baltimore, MD: Johns Hopkins University Press, 2009). His opinion editorials appear on the website of the Strategic Studies Institute; his most recent contribution was, "What Our Civilian Leaders Do Not Understand about the Ethic of Military Professions: A Striking Example of the Current Gap in Civil-Military Relations." Dr. Snider holds M.A. degrees in economics and public policy from the University of Wisconsin and a Ph.D. in public policy from the University of Maryland.

ALEXANDER P. SHINE is a retired U.S. Army Colonel and educator. His military service included tours of duty in Korea and Vietnam, infantry command at the company and battalion level, and teaching assignments at the U.S. Military Academy, New York (U.S. History); Wheaton College, IL (Military Science); and the U.S. Army War College (National Security Strategy). Following retirement from the Army, he served a decade as Commandant of Cadets and Professor of History at Culver Military Academy in Culver, IN. Colonel Shine currently does contract editing for the Strategic Studies Institute and teaches about World War II and the Civil War for a travel agency. His articles have appeared in *Command, Infantry, Air Power Journal, Parameters,* and *Armed Forces Journal.* Colonel Shine holds a B.S. from the U.S. Military Academy and an M.A. in history from Harvard University.

SUMMARY

The context for this monograph lies in the trust relationships that American military professions must retain with the society they serve if they are to remain professions. Of course, the alternative without such trust is for the Services simply to revert to the character and behavior of a government occupation, a big bureaucracy like the Internal Revenue Service or the Department of Agriculture. But to remain professions, one of the constant challenges the Stewards of the Professions must address is "how different and how separate" they are to be from the society they serve. Stated differently, as the values and mores of American society change, the ethics of its military professions must also evolve, but never so much that such evolution diminishes their military effectiveness — their *raison-d'être* and the source of the trust relationship in the first place.

As noted in the Foreword, as the values of American society have changed in the past, in most cases, e.g., racial integration, abortion, smoking as a health issue, the service of gays in the military, gender roles, etc., those changes have eventually had a strong influence on the culture of the military professions and, in particular, on the core of those cultures — the Services' Ethics.

The authors of this monograph argue that another such issue has now arisen and is strongly, and not favorably, influencing military cultures — a culture of hostility toward religion and its correct expressions within the military. Setting aside the role of Chaplains as a separate issue, the focus here is on the role religion may play in the moral character of individual soldiers, especially leaders, and how their personal morality, faith-based or not, is to be integrated with their profession's ethic so they can serve in all cases "without reservation," as their oath requires.

The authors assert, with cogent examples, that Service cultures have become increasingly hostile to the correct expressions of religion, perhaps to the point that soldiers of faith are now intimidated into privatizing their beliefs . . . and thus serving hypocritically as someone other than who they really are. If the Services really want leaders "of character" as their doctrines so plainly state, then they must maintain professional cultures that allow, indeed foster, authentic moral character whether faith-based or not, and its development as soldiers volunteer and serve. The Services can ill afford to lose the irrefutable power of soldiers' personal moralities as they serve in both peace and in war, providing an additional motivation and resilience to prevail in the arduous tasks and inevitable recoveries inherent in their sacrificial service.

After advancing this hypothesis and viewing it from several perspectives, the authors then move downward in hierarchy to address the service they know best—the U.S. Army—and offer recommendations for both Soldiers and the Stewards of the Army Profession as to the best way to maintain such a professional culture. The intent clearly is to start a discussion within the profession on an issue that the Army, at least, has placed for too long in the "too hard" box.

A SOLDIER'S MORALITY, RELIGION, AND OUR PROFESSIONAL ETHIC: DOES THE ARMY'S CULTURE FACILITATE INTEGRATION, CHARACTER DEVELOPMENT, AND TRUST IN THE PROFESSION?

INTRODUCTION

In October 2013, the Secretary of the Army directed a halt to all "briefings, command presentations, or training on the subject of extremist organizations until that program of instruction and training has been [re]created and disseminated." The Secretary acted because:

> On several occasions over the past few months, media accounts have highlighted instances of Army instructors supplementing programs of instruction and including information that is inaccurate, objectionable, and otherwise inconsistent with current Army policy.[1]

Of interest is the fact that during those briefings, Catholics, Evangelical Christians, and several apolitical religious advocacy groups in Washington, DC, had been labeled by Army instructors as "hate groups." News of this drew negative reaction from members of Congress who strongly addressed their concerns to the Secretary.[2]

How could such unprofessional conduct on the part of Army instructors happen "on several occasions over the past few months" without, apparently, corrective action being taken by uniformed leaders at each location, or even at some higher uniformed level? Why did they stand on the sidelines so long that it took the Secretary of the Army to act? Why did they not recognize what the Secretary did—that such representations are "inaccurate, objectionable, and otherwise inconsistent with Army policy," not to mention, common sense?

On November 18, 2013, the American Civil Liberties Union (ACLU) commended the Secretary by letter for his action noting that:

> . . . to the extent these trainings served to dissuade personnel from engaging in lawful associational or expressive activities, they raise serious concerns under the First Amendment . . . jeopardize[ing] other important Army goals and values.

In an accompanying news article, the same ACLU authors further noted:

> The Army did the right thing in halting these trainings until it can get a handle on the curriculum to prevent inaccuracies and ensure that they properly further the program's goals of treating everyone with dignity and respect. **No soldier should fear repercussions because of their personal beliefs. The men and women who volunteer to defend the Constitution deserve its protections, including freedom of association and religion and belief, as well as fair treatment and equal opportunity for everyone.**[3] (bold added by authors of this monograph)

We contend that this example, one of several that we shall discuss, highlights a much larger issue — that the Army's professional culture, as well as those of the other Services, has become increasingly hostile to almost any expression of personal moralities — and particularly those based on religion — so hostile that citizens can rightly wonder whether the conduct of the institutions continues to reflect the legal and moral foundations of the professions' own ethics. Put another way, in a national culture and political milieu wherein an individual's personal morality, particularly when it is based on religion, is increasingly contested, can the Services maintain professional cultures that foster the legitimacy of service and sacrifice by men and women of religious faith—or, indeed of no faith—who choose to think, speak, and act, within prescribed limits in accordance with their own personal morality? Can they serve, as noted by the ACLU, without "fear of repercussions because of their personal beliefs . . . enjoying freedom of association and religion and belief as well as fair treatment and equal opportunity?"

It is our understanding that every Soldier has a personal morality that starts with what he or she believes to be good, right, and just. More specifically, it is:

> . . . the worldview component of one's human spirit, or personal essence. This system of beliefs defines who a person is, what the person stands for, serves as a guide for determining behavior—especially in ambiguous and chaotic situations—and also provides the courage and will to act in accordance with one's beliefs and values.[4]

In the doctrines of the Army, this is known as the Soldier's character, a leader attribute that is to be marked by integrity, consistently "doing what is right legally and morally."[5] At a time in the Army's history when failures caused by lack of individual and institutional character abound—with sexual assault and sexual harassment at the top of the list—this issue could hardly be more important to our leaders.

Understood this way, we believe this issue now presents a direct challenge to the Stewards of our military professions: Can they adapt professional cultures to attract, motivate, and retain volunteers of moral

3

character—including those religiously based—that are compatible with the professions' ethics, thus enabling our armed forces to remain militarily effective and ethical, earning the trust of those serving as well as that of the American people?

BACKGROUND AND CONTEXT

> Congress shall make no law respecting an establishment of religion, or prohibiting the free exercise thereof; or abridging the freedom of speech, or of the press; or the right of the people to peaceably assemble, and to petition the Government for a redress of grievances.
>
> First Amendment to the U.S. Constitution

> Everyone has the right to freedom of thought, conscience, and religion; this right includes freedom to change his religion or belief, and freedom, either alone or in community with others and in public or private, to manifest his religion or belief in teaching, practice, worship and observance.
>
> Universal Declaration of Human Rights, Article 18, United Nations, 1948

The two epigraphs above provide context for this monograph. As they indicate, Americans are privileged, indeed. They enjoy human rights and history teaches us that, elsewhere in the world, others have only aspired to this level of privilege. Among those, as the First Amendment to our Constitution states, they are free to enjoy the priceless liberty of conscience, and with it, the choice of what belief system to follow, religious or nonreligious. Further, as the second epigraph notes, this is not just an American ideal; it is our aspiration in concert with like-minded nations for all of mankind.

4

Soldiers[6] of the nation's military professions have sacrificed much blood, indeed life, over the 2+ centuries of the Republic's existence to safeguard its liberty, and with it, the exercise by its citizens of these individual liberties of conscience and belief, including those that are founded on religion. They have also sacrificed in the cause of extending these liberties to citizens of other nations, increasingly so in the last several decades. Because of these sacrifices, military professionals have an abiding interest in the exercise of these liberties, both by themselves and those they defend.

However, it is also true that soldiers in service to the Republic give up some of their rights as American citizens for the necessities of an effective and ethical military profession. The regulations of the Departments of Defense (DoD) and the Army state the applicable policies:

> The U.S. Constitution proscribes Congress from enacting any law prohibiting the free exercise of religion. The Department of Defense places a high value on the rights of members of the Military Services to observe the tenets of their respective religions. It is DoD policy that requests for accommodation of religious practices should be approved by commanders when accommodation will not have an adverse impact on mission accomplishment, military readiness, unit cohesion, standards, or discipline.
>
> Department of Defense Instruction Number 1300.17, February 10, 2009[7]

> The Army places a high value on the rights of its Soldiers to observe tenets of their respective religious faiths. The Army will approve requests for accommodation of religious practices unless accommodation

5

will have an adverse impact on unit readiness, individual readiness, unit cohesion, morale, discipline, safety, and/or health. As used in this regulation, these factors will be referred to individually and collectively as 'military necessity' unless otherwise stated. Accommodation of a Soldier's religious practices must be examined against military necessity and cannot be guaranteed at all times.

> Army Regulation 600-20, Army Command Policy, September 2012, para 5-6, Accommodating religious practices[8]

So the enduring challenge facing the leaders of the Army and the other Services is how to balance the restrictions placed on soldiers' practice of their liberties—due to what the Army in its regulation calls "military necessity"—with their constitutional rights to hold religious beliefs as the basis of their personal morality and to exercise those beliefs as acts of conscience. How do the Stewards of the Professions establish that necessary balance within the professions' cultures such that uniformed leaders actually lead with confidence and sensitivity on issues of religion and its expression within their units and commands? Serving under oath to "support and defend the Constitution of the United States," it is logical that young professionals expect their leaders to achieve such balance within the culture of the military professions in which they have volunteered to serve.

Two additional points of perspective need to be included in this section. First, we note that there exists in military professions a mutual responsibility for the moral development—or character development, in doctrinal language—of individual professionals. On the one hand, it is the responsibility of individual leaders within the profession of arms to integrate their personal morality, faith-based or not, with the ethic of their vocation such that they can always execute their military duties "without reservation," as their oath states. In our own case at least, this was not too difficult, including for each of us who participated in multiple combat tours as leaders in the infantry. But we served at a different time, one where there was less concern than there is today about a Soldier's personal morality, and there was not the undercurrent of hostility to religious expression that we address in this monograph.

On the other hand, as we will more fully explain in subsequent sections, the profession shares responsibility for a leader's character development, including his or her successful integration of personal morality with professional ethic. It does so by ensuring that the culture and practices of the institution are not hostile to, or intimidating of, the leaders' correct expressions of his or her personal morality, whether faith based or not. This is the ". . . no soldier should fear repercussions because of their personal beliefs . . ." of the ACLU discussed earlier. We will discuss this shared responsibility further in Section II.

Second, we note that, while we will address this issue of cultural intimidation within the context of America's military professions, their ethics, and their leaders, it is also of current interest to other disciplines whose inquiries are germane to our discussion. In particular, among political theorists, moral philosophers, and military ethicists, there has been a lengthy debate over the applicability of the **doctrine of religious restraint** to decisionmaking within liberal democracies. Originally construed to address the proper public role of religion—and more particularly the role religion should play as citizens and elected political officials employ their modicum of political power within a pluralistic, liberal democracy — the doctrine held that religion should not play a decisive role in their choices as to which candidates or policies to support. In short, it is fair to say the doctrine advocates, in essence, that citizens and their elected politicians privatize their religious convictions in their roles as voters or public servants.[9]

Over the years, the doctrine of religious restraint has remained contentious because many Americans do not accept a distinction between what is morally correct and what is religiously correct; to them, the two are not separable within their world view. They dispute the claim of the doctrine toward privatization of their religious views on the grounds that, in fulfilling their public roles, they (citizens and politicians) should not be denied the grounds (religious) on which to decide the best (morally best) policies and positions to take.

More recently, this debate has been extended to the applicability of the doctrine to the role of military professionals, and particularly to uniformed leaders with command authority. Of interest to our discussion here, two members of the faculty at the U.S. Naval Academy have recently argued against extension of the doctrine of religious restraint to military decisionmaking. They argue that, just as a citizen ought to support those public policies that he or she believes to be morally correct, so a soldier has a role-specific moral obligation to make only those professional judgments that he or she sincerely believes to be morally correct. And if, for a particular leader of religious faith, the most morally correct discretionary judgment is one based on his or her personal, faith-based morality, then it should be made on that basis. They offer a new doctrine:

Call this understanding *The Doctrine of Conscientious Action* (DCA): where the relevant legal and statutory constraints leave room for a soldier's discretionary judgment, then he should use his discretion in a morally responsible manner. He should try to use his discretion in such a way as to get right moral, legal, and operational results. Given the lack of a principled normative difference between the religious and the moral, it follows that he should use his discretion to get the right religious result as well. Given the demographics of the United States, a 'moral' military is at one and the same time a religious military.[10]

As we shall see, given the increases in ethnic diversity and religious pluralism amid a larger trend of secularization that is American society today, the challenge to maintain within our military professions a culture in which personal moralities can be motivational, including those which are religion based, is a challenge of increasing intensity and importance. Our intent in this monograph, then, is to articulate perspectives, analyses, and recommendations that will help civilian and military leaders within the Army and the other Services address this challenge.

We will proceed from here in five sections: First, we will highlight further the growing culture of hostility toward religious expression within the Services. Second, narrowing the focus of the monograph to the Service we know best, the U.S. Army, we will place this issue in the context of the profession's meritocratic ethic and its use by leaders of all ranks to self-police the military's culture and behavior. Third, we will offer our perspective of how leaders within the Army whose personal morality is based on religious faith see this growing issue. Fourth, we will present a brief analysis of options to address the issue; and then, fifth, we will offer brief recommendations from an Army perspective.

I. THE EVOLVING CULTURE OF HOSTILITY TOWARD RELIGIOUS PRESENCE AND EXPRESSION

As discussed briefly in the introduction, we believe that over the past 2 decades, coincident with the growing secularization of American society, the culture of our Armed Services has become more hostile to many things religious, including religious expression by individuals in uniform and the application of any sort of religious basis for decisionmaking. This has created, in perception or reality, a culture hostile to, and perhaps even intimidating for, serving soldiers of religious faith.

We also note that this trend of increasing hostility to religious expression within our Armed Services is not an isolated trend and is not surprising since there are at least three well-recognized societal trends that are occurring along with it:[11] First, the general secularization of American society and the cultural wars that this has created over the past several decades; second, the activism of several legal advocacy groups specifically hostile to religious expression within the military; and third, the advancement of America's cultural wars into the military, particularly by political advocates/reformers focused on individual issues.

Turning now to examples of such hostility to religious expression, we offer the following instances:[12]

- September 2011: Air Force Chief of Staff General Norton Schwartz issued a Service-wide memo entitled, "Maintaining Government Neutrality Regarding Religion." It states, "Leaders at all levels must balance constitutional protections for an individual's free exercise of religion or other personal beliefs and its prohibition against governmental establishment of religion." For example, they must avoid the "actual or apparent" use of their position to promote their personal religious beliefs to their subordinates. "Commanders . . . who engage in such behavior may cause members to doubt their impartiality and objectivity. The potential result is a degradation of the unit's morale, good order and discipline." General Schwartz also warned commanders against open support of chaplain-run events, stating that they "must refrain from appearing to officially endorse religion generally or any particular religion. Therefore, I expect chaplains, not commanders, to notify Airmen of Chaplain Corps programs."[13] Finally, Schwartz advised anyone who has concerns "involving the preservation of government neutrality regarding religious beliefs" to contact a military attorney.

From our perspective, the threatening tone of the final comment is obvious. So is the excessive concern over "apparent" use of commanders' positions to promote their religious beliefs, and the concern that commanders who are known to be religious may, more than those with other world views, cause subordinates to doubt their impartiality and objectivity. Further, we believe that by precluding commanders from even speaking about the "Chaplain Corps programs" in their own units, such activities, as well as the silenced commanders, are marginalized in the eyes of the very Airmen they have sworn to lead and develop. Ironically, commanders may advertise, and indeed encourage attendance at any number of voluntary functions but not those of a religious nature, even in cases where they personally believe the function would be desired by, and could be of significant developmental benefit to, many of their Airmen. Such "over the top" reactions by senior military leaders to the cultural intimidation they are facing serve, sadly, as the basis for construal by junior professionals that if they "lead-up" in such situations, they will be seen as insubordinate. Intimidation begets intimidation, eviscerating professional culture.

- September 2011: Walter Reed National Military Medical Center, the leading medical institution for the U.S. Armed Forces, issued an official patient and visitor policy banning Bibles (to our understanding the ban was imposed only on Bibles, rather than such authoritative writings of all major faith groups). It stated, "No religious items (i.e., Bibles, reading material, and/or artifacts) are allowed to be given away or used during a visit." The policy was revoked after a political firestorm erupted in the House of Representatives,[14] but its intent cannot be missed. Neither can the fact that such intent runs utterly contrary to decades of understanding within the military professions of the positive role that religion and its various expressions play in the fitness of soldiers for mortal combat and subsequent recovery from combat-related sacrifices.[15]

- May 2013: The DoD issued the following statement:

  > The U.S. Department of Defense has never and will never single out a particular religious group for persecution or prosecution. . . . Service members can share their faith (evangelize), but must not force unwanted, intrusive attempts to convert others of any faith or no faith to one's beliefs (proselytization).[16]

  If religious expression within military cultures was not at issue, then why was such a directive needed?

- June 2013: The House Armed Services Committee adopted an amendment by Representative John Fleming (R-LA) to the National Defense Authorization Act (NDAA). The Fleming Amendment seeks to ensure protection of the rights of Armed Services members to hold, act upon, and practice freely their religious beliefs as long as they do not interfere with any constitutional liberties of others. As Representative Fleming notes in his press release:

  > . . .troubling reports indicate that the military may be focused only on protecting beliefs of service members and not the exercise or expression of those beliefs. My amendment is necessary to ensure that men and women of faith will not be discriminated against in the Armed Forces, and will be free to exercise their religious beliefs.[17]

- June 2013: President Barack Obama objected to the Fleming amendment. On June 11, after the

House Armed Services Committee approved its version of the NDAA (H.R. 1960) with Representative Fleming's language, a White House Statement of Administration Policy was issued, indicating that the President's senior advisers would recommend a veto because they strongly objected:

> to section 530, which would require the Armed Forces to accommodate, except in cases of military necessity, 'actions and speech' reflecting the 'conscience, moral principles, or religious beliefs of the member.' By limiting the discretion of commanders to address potentially problematic speech and actions within their units, this provision would have significant adverse effect on good order, discipline, morale, and mission accomplishment.[18]

But, why would the President's advisors recommend he veto legislation based exactly on the "military necessity" language in the DoD and Service policies; unless, that is, they did not want accommodation of such actions and speech?

We conclude from these examples that the institutional behavior of our military professions within the DoD manifests cultures that can fairly be described as increasingly hostile to personal moralities and their rightful expression, especially when based on religion. While this is deleterious today to ethical military professions, we must also be mindful of the second order effects occurring in the current development of junior professionals. Simply stated, they take their cues from those above them, making their decisions based on their construal of senior leaders' priorities, values, guidance, etc. They correctly see the need for everybody in the organization to get on board with current policy. But our concern is that they may then equate dissent or difference in belief with insubordination. If junior leaders make that type of construal regarding their obligations to senior officers and lack the experiences to see the value to the profession of a rich array of personal beliefs (even those that may lead to conflict between soldiers), then they will be more likely to establish in the future their own command climates wherein religion and its influences on character development are not encouraged and perhaps not even welcomed.

While much of the hostility has been directed at the Chaplains' Corps of our Armed Services, we have excluded all such examples (which are, in fact, far more numerous than those offered here) since the Chaplains' Corps are not the focus of this monograph. We focus instead on the challenge this cultural hostility presents to the Stewards of our military professions as well as to both uniformed and civilian leaders of all ranks within them whose personal morality is based on one of the world's major religious faiths.

II. THE ARMY'S PROFESSIONAL MILITARY ETHIC

While we have addressed the culture of hostility toward religious expression as it exists throughout the DoD, our focus now shifts downward in hierarchy to the Department of the Army. Here our analysis will focus on the Army as a military profession that, like all professions, uses its ethic as the primary means of

15

social control over institutional policies as well as over its personnel and their professional work.

Fortunately for this discussion, the Army has very recently (June 2013) officially articulated for the first time its understanding of itself as a military profession: *Army Doctrine Reference Publication No. 1, (ADRP1), The Army Profession.*[19] Included in the new doctrine is a significant discussion on the leader's role in building and maintaining trust—the central organizing principle of the profession—by adherence to the Army's Ethic. That discussion includes a framework for integrating and understanding the many different components of the Army's Ethic.[20] (See Figure 1.)

	Legal Foundations (*codified*)	Moral Foundations
Army as Profession *(Laws/values/norms for performance of collective institution)*	**Legal-Institutional** The U.S. Constitution Titles 5, 10, 32, U.S. Code Treaties of which U.S. is party Status-of-Forces Agreements Law of Armed Conflict	**Moral-Institutional** The U.S. Declaration of Independence Just War Tradition Trust Relationships of the Profession

Individual as Professional *(Laws/values/norms for performance of individual prodessionals)*	**Legal-Individual**
	 Oath of:
	   Enlistment
	   Commision
	   Office
	 U.S. Code - Standards of
	   Exemplary Conduct
	 UCMJ
	 Rules of Engagement
	 Soldier's Rules
		Moral-Individual
		 Universal Norms:
		   Basic Rights
		   Golden Rule
		 Values, Creeds, and Mottos:
		   "Duty, Honor, Country"
		   NCO Creed, Civilian Creed
		   7 Army Values
		   Soldier's Creed
		   Warrior Ethos

NCO - noncommissioned officer
U.S. - United States
UCMJ - Uniform Code of Military Justice

Figure 1. The Framework of the Army Ethic.

While it is beyond the scope of this monograph to present the Army Ethic completely, four aspects of it are of interest to the issue we are addressing:

1. **The Ethic has two foundations — legal and moral**. Since the inception of the Army in 1775, its ethic has had both legal (codified) and moral foundations. War, the practice of the Army Profession by its brutal nature, has long been viewed as a vexing moral challenge. Over the centuries, nations have sought to legitimize some acts of war under certain conditions and to delegitimize others, to constrain the horrors of war as well as the peacetime behavior of martial institutions, by legal code. As the framework shows, these constraints apply today to the Army as an institution, as well as to individual Soldiers, in peace and in war. But there are also the moral foundations of our ethic, which apply in similar manner to both the institution and individual professionals. Of importance to this monograph is the recognition that Soldiers are to be aware that their personal morality, their views on the "Universal Norms" — what they personally believe to be good, right, and just — are to be considered and integrated with other legal and moral norms of interpersonal behavior as they live their lives and fulfill their professional responsibilities. Army professionals are to live and act each day based on **both** the legal and moral foundations of the profession's ethic, and a part of those moral norms is their personal morality. No Army professional is ever asked to give up his or her personal morality to become a Soldier; rather their task is integration with the profession's ethic in order to serve and lead with personal integrity (see further discussion on Aspect 4 later in the monograph).

2. **The Motivations of the Army Ethic**. As the new doctrine explicates, each of these sets of ethical founda-

tions, legal and moral, tend to produce different forms of motivation in Army professionals. The legal norms produce the motivation of obligation (I have taken an oath and I **must** do my duty, or I am in violation of my oath and will be punished under the Uniform Code of Military Justice for dereliction of those duties). In contrast, the motivation produced under the moral norms is that of aspiration (I **want** to do what is right, both legally and morally, because that is what I believe in; it is who I am now and who I am becoming in the future; it authentically reflects my personal character and values and reflects why I am an Army professional).[21] While both forms of motivation have their uses, it is common sense, as well as Army doctrine, to prefer transformational leadership that draws on the moral foundations and inspires Army professionals to honorable service over motivation that is based punitively on law and regulations.[22]

3. **The Meritocratic Essence of the Army Ethic based on Certifications by the "three C's" of Competence, Character, and Commitment.** All professions seek to create and maintain a culture, with their ethic at its core, that places extremely high value on the institution's behavior as a meritocracy. For the Army, this means advancement based on individual merit alone, with no partiality shown to any individual or group. Professions thus ensure that only practitioners fully qualified in competence, character, and commitment are advanced to positions of higher responsibility and service to their client. This is how professions remain effective in their expert work, which in turn maintains the trust of their client—which is the lifeblood of the profession's existence. Maintaining this essence of their cultural and ethical foundation explains why all professions, including the Army, place

such importance on repetitive certification of their individual professionals. Preferential treatment in certifications, or any other benefit of being a member of the profession, is taboo; all must be earned strictly on the basis of individually demonstrated merit.

4. **Integration of personal morality with the ethic of the profession is required for Army leaders to be self-aware and integral, and thus authentic leaders "of character."** Army doctrine on leadership is informative here:

> Leadership is affected by a person's character and identity. Integrity is a key mark of a leader's character. It means doing what is right, legally and morally. . . . Leaders of integrity adhere to the values that are a part of their personal identity and set a standard for their followers to emulate. Identity is one's self-concept, how one defines himself or herself. . . . [23]

This understanding of authentic leadership — leading by accurately reflecting in words and actions who you are holistically as a person — places the responsibility on the individual professional to integrate his or her personal morality with the other components of the Army's Ethic, legal and moral, and then to lead consistently from that identity. Army leaders may not identify themselves as one person on duty and another off duty; their character, if authentically displayed, will vary little from situation to situation. Living and leading from an identity that is not integrated, meaning one that places one's personal morality outside the scope of professional ethics, drawing then on each one on a situational basis, does not comport with Army leadership doctrines and will quickly be recognized by followers as inauthentic. In stark contrast, recent research from Iraq again establishes that in combat, authentic military leaders have high impacts on their followers.[24]

We conclude this section by noting again that new Army doctrine reaffirms a mutual responsibility, shared between individual professionals and the Army Profession for the development of professionals and their adaptation and implementation of the ethic as a means of social control.[25] Put simply, to be an authentic person of character, the individual Soldier and leader must live, on and off duty, consistently with his or her understanding of right and wrong—the individual integration of personal morality and the professional ethic. If it becomes impossible for a Soldier to do so because of hostility to liberty of conscience and legitimate religious expression, then he or she must make a choice (which we will discuss in Section IV).

Before that occurs, however, to fulfill its part of the mutual responsibility, the institution—the Stewards of the Army Profession—must make every effort consistent with mission effectiveness to avoid such individual-institutional ethical conflicts. Thus, to reiterate the challenge we are discussing in this monograph: **The enduring challenge facing the leaders of the Army and the other Services is how to balance the restrictions placed on soldiers' practice of their liberties—due to what the Army in its regulation calls "military necessity"—with their constitutional rights to hold religious beliefs as the basis of their personal morality and to exercise those beliefs as acts of conscience.**

III. THE CHALLENGE AND OPPORTUNITIES TO THE LEADER OF RELIGIOUS FAITH

As discussed briefly in the introduction and in the previous paragraph, the challenge to the leader of religious faith, regardless of rank, is that of integrating one's personal morality with the profession's ethic in order to be a leader of authenticity, not compartmenting a life of faith from a life of service to the Republic.[26] Challenges arise because personal moralities based on a religious faith are considered by most adherents to be the higher calling, and thus to take precedence on occasion over a vocational or professional ethic or directive, whether actual or perceived. They can also arise because such moralities generally prohibit compartmentalization of one's life into personal and vocational spheres, just as Army leadership doctrine requires authenticity and wholeness of one's character (as discussed in Section II). Instead, integrity and authenticity as a person of faith is required in all roles in life, often requiring a religious presence and expression. Thus, in the event of a clash between a Soldier's personal morality and his or her understanding of responsibility under the Army's Ethic or directives, he or she cannot in good conscience simply jettison the personal ethic to support that of the Army.

Even with these two conditions, however, actual clashes have until recently been rare. But the growing hostility towards religious expression or religious-based ethical decisions has, unfortunately and largely unnecessarily, brought such clashes to the fore. In this section, we present a few specific, recent examples of real or potential clashes emanating from the culture of hostility to religious expression.

January 24, 2013, Army Removes Cross and Steeple from Chapel.

The U.S. military ordered Soldiers to take down a steeple and board up the cross-shaped windows of a chapel at remote Forward Operating Base Orgun-E in Afghanistan. The Soldiers were told the chapel must remain religiously neutral. In 2011, a similar situation occurred where Soldiers were forced to remove a cross at a chapel at Camp Marmal, Afghanistan.[27]

While there may have been legitimate concerns that Christian symbols visible to the outside could be unnecessarily inflammatory in the context of the particular conflict in Afghanistan, what is particularly disturbing in this instance is the rationale given for the decision; this example highlights how far a policy of "neutrality" toward religion can overstep into traditional and legitimate expression of a particular religious faith group. Historically, houses of worship built with appropriated dollars within the military services have accommodated the need of the Judeo-Christian faith groups, and they are now expanding to accommodate the religious expression of other faith groups, e.g., Muslim. At the time of a religious service of a particular faith group, should not the house of worship reflect the essential icons and artifacts of that particular group?

Conflict between the Leader of Faith's Commitment to Objective Truth and Truth-Telling and the Institution's Tendency to Sacrifice such Truth and Truth-Telling for Perceived Positive Outcomes for the Army.

There has always been pressure within the military as well as other large institutions to sacrifice objective truth for expediency, a storyline more palatable but less than the full truth.[28] Clearly, the culture extent in the Army today that requires extensive use of the Article 15-6, UCMJ, formal investigations, feeds this pressure.[29]

In a recent example reported by an officer in Afghanistan, two Army majors were found, via Article 15-6 investigations, to be responsible for the deaths of Soldiers in their units even though the investigator of the incident had not even queried the majors before passing his conclusions up the chain of command.[30] To believe in objective truth suggests that the report should have stated that, though mistakes had been made, they were honest mistakes in a complex and chaotic situation and most likely were made by one of the dead Soldiers, and the actions (or inactions) of the majors were, at worst, a minor contributing factor. However, the culture of the command led the investigating officer to conclude that such a finding would be insensitive to the surviving family members of the dead NCO, and therefore the command sought to find someone else accountable amid the complexities of the situation. Finding someone responsible (other than one of the dead Soldiers) got the command off the hook and presumably kept the issue from blowing up into something bigger, which could have been damaging to the Army and distracting to the larger mission. Such situations are not uncommon, and there are sometimes apparently good reasons for sacrificing objective truth for a "spin" that seems to serve broader strategic or institutional purposes in the short term.

However, as the incident of Army Specialist Patrick Tillman and so many others have shown over the past decade of war, the short-term gain from sacrificing objective truth for some perceived higher good is inconsistent with the Army's Ethic and most often causes much bigger problems later.[31] Because of the strong admonitions against dishonesty in religious teachings, Soldiers of religious faith will find it **particularly** difficult to sacrifice objective truth even for short-term expediency, unit morale, or perceived institutional gains.[32] As such, their approach of "wait a minute, never be content with a half-truth when the whole can be won," may be just what is needed to check the institutional temptation to sacrifice truth for a more palatable institutional spin.

Supporting an Annual DoD-Sponsored Gay Pride Month.

In simple terms, the DoD report for implementation of the repeal of the "Don't Ask Don't Tell" (DADT) policy recommended that soldiers be treated as soldiers, with dignity and respect based on performance without regard to their sexual orientation.[33] But, in making their recommendations, the report authors (Honorable Jeh Charles Johnson and Army General F. Carter Ham) were also careful to note the sincerely held "moral and religious objections to homosexuality" of a significant number of service members.[34] Regarding these beliefs, they stated:

> In the course of our review, we heard a large number of Service members raise religious and moral objections to homosexuality and to serving with someone who is gay. Some feared repeal of [DADT] might limit their individual freedom of expression and free exercise of religion, or require them to change their personal beliefs about the morality of homosexuality. The views expressed to us in these terms cannot be downplayed or dismissed.[35]

In a later part of the report, the authors further made it clear that "We do *not* [emphasis in original] recommend that sexual orientation be placed alongside race, color, religion, sex, and national origin as a class eligible for various diversity programs. . . ."[36]

In their recommendations, the authors were recognizing something that we believe is now being ignored in the follow-on designation by the DoD in June of each year as "Gay Pride Month." Not all religious Americans consider homosexual behavior to be in violation of their own moral understandings, but many, including within the military, do so for reasons arguably consistent with the theology of their religion. In finally allowing gay soldiers to serve openly without prejudice, the DoD is rightly saying to all soldiers and their leaders that they must **accommodate** gay soldiers without prejudice regarding their nonduty-related behavior. But in establishing an officially sponsored "Gay Pride" month with related publicity and public functions, the DoD is requiring (or at least strongly encouraging) those soldiers who object on moral grounds to homosexual practices to not just **accommodate** gay soldiers, but to join in the institutional **endorsement and celebration** of homosexual behavior. That, many soldiers of religious faith cannot in good conscience do, and we argue they should not be asked to do so.

As can be seen from these examples, for many individuals, their reaction to an increasing number of situations may be particularly intense because of the strength of their personal faith-based beliefs. This can be expected to create critical moral dilemmas for these Soldiers, especially those responsible for leading and developing others, when conflicts arise between their personal conscience and the orders or ethical demands of their work. However, experience has taught us that, for every challenge, there is also an opportunity. In this case, it is the opportunity that is available to all leaders, regardless of personal morality, to leverage Soldiers' personal beliefs and practices in their professional development and in the development of the climate and culture of the entire organization. We address how the leaders of the Army Profession can address these opportunities in Section IV.

IV. OPPORTUNITIES FOR LEADERS OF RELIGIOUS FAITH

Some have responded that there should be no moral dilemma for Soldiers in such circumstances. Simply stated, in their view, the law rules — volunteers, religious or not, should park their personal morality at the door when they take their oath. We designate this as the legalist view, one which holds that all Soldiers, regardless of personal morality, should simply reconsider their legal obligations as laid out in the Constitution, Federal statutes such as Title 10, their Oath of Service and their Service's regulations, and do what the law requires. In this view, the Army has no responsibility to preclude or attempt to resolve moral dilemmas other than to keep the legal foundations of its ethic current to the official mandates of the public it serves.[37]

Perhaps too narrowly characterized, there are nonetheless two obvious difficulties with this view. First, it does not address the dilemma created by recent policies and orders that the leader of religious faith believes to be immoral; in other words, it fails to understand, as discussed in Section II, that the profession's ethic has moral as well as legal foundations, and that the moral foundation is an essential element of the character of every Soldier and leader of Soldiers. Second, it fails to recognize, also discussed earlier, that the institution does have developmental responsibilities, shared with the individual professional, for preclusion of such moral dilemmas to the extent possible and for their prompt resolution, should they occur.

Contrary to the legalist view, as we see it, there are three opportunities for Soldiers of religious faith when facing what they perceive to be a conflict between their religion-based personal morality and what the institution is expecting of them:

1. They may choose to compromise their religion-based convictions so as to go along with the prevailing institutional/cultural view. In doing so, however, they will be inauthentic to their core values and thus dishonest; they will be leaders without integrity. They become compartmented leaders and, by their actions, also encourage others to do the same. Lack of integrity in dealing with a known ethical dilemma, particularly by an Army leader, whose every decision and action is carefully watched by his or her followers, will lead to lack of integrity and/or trust by the followers.

2. They may continue to serve honorably within the Army Profession, but in order to maintain their integrity they will work within the institution to preclude and resolve such moral dilemmas. In other words, they are to get off of the sidelines and "lead-up," actively engaging and assisting the Stewards of the Profession in their vital role of maintaining, over time, both the effectiveness and the ethical standing of the Army Profession.[38] We will return to this theme in our recommendations section.

3. The Soldier of religious faith could leave the military profession, having decided, presumably, that the cost of compromising one's personal integrity is

27

too high a price to pay to continue in sacrificial service to the Republic. The tragic loss to the Army and to the Republic of such integrated men and women of character, many with well over a decade of distinguished service in combat, leads logically to a discussion of why this opportunity is to be earnestly avoided by both the individuals and by the Army.

Why Not Just Let Soldiers of Religious Faith Leave the Army?

Our first response to this question is because it is right that the U.S. Army be an institution that as closely as possible reflects the values of the nation it serves. Stated differently, this is the issue of political legitimacy of the institution — Does the Army accurately reflect within its ranks the society that trusts it for security?[39] One of the most fundamental of those values is our freedom of belief and conscience and the exercise of conscience which often springs from, and is informed by, a religious faith. American citizens should be free, and feel free, to join the Army, expecting rightly that if their personal morality is faith-based, that fact is not in any way a hindrance to service. When such freedoms are to be restricted by the Army for "military necessity" (see the discussion in the Background section), there should be strong, compelling reasons for doing so, reasons that go beyond current social and cultural trends or the fear that one Soldier's beliefs may be in conflict with the beliefs or practices of another Soldier.[40]

Our second response is that the Army has now, once again, the opportunity to lead our nation. In the midst of the stifling cultural wars within American society, wars of mutual disrespect toward citizens who have strong differences on issues that matter to them, the Army can set an example as it has consistently — if imperfectly — done on other issues. The example should be that, for purposes of military effectiveness, the Army is and will continue to be a professional meritocracy. In such a noble institution, Soldiers work together, treat each other with dignity and respect, openly express their deeply held views, and, regardless of differences, evaluate each others' performances based on the certifications and other standards of the profession, not on their views about ideas and practices not directly related to those duties. This is pluralism, multi-culturalism, and diversity rightly leveraged for military effectiveness!

Further, we believe that a culture increasingly hostile toward religious expression will eventually cause some number of good Soldiers of all ranks to leave the Army. A Soldier seriously committed to his or her personal morality, whether grounded in a religious faith or not, is prone more than he or she would otherwise be to live up to the high ethical ideals of the Army Profession **not in spite of, but because of** his or her personal convictions. For those who ground their convictions in the tenets of the major religions, virtually all emphasize the values of altruism (selfless service); truth-telling; integrity; respect for others; personal humility; moral and physical courage; to mention only some of the personal virtues valuable, indeed necessary, in military professions.

As most all behaviorists agree (if they agree on anything), while it is sometimes difficult to **know** what is right, it is always far more difficult to **do** what is right. It is certainly true that the strength of character of an Army professional **is always on display** in the crucible of making decisions and taking actions to implement those decisions. In such situations, Soldiers of religious faith are motivated more by aspiration than by obligation; they have a strong intrinsic motivation, which reinforces that of the military, to be the leader the Services need them to be and whose actions manifest their personal character with integrity. Religious ethics, then, are a strong **reinforcer** of military ethics. In our view, it will be self-defeating for the Army to cause men and women imbued with this reinforcing ethical framework to leave the Army because it allowed a culture hostile or intimidating to their beliefs, conscience, and expression of those beliefs.

Finally, and perhaps most importantly, it is simply indisputable that religion is often a key element in the emotional and psychological health of individual Soldiers. While the Army and the other Services have recently struggled with just how to understand and present this spiritual domain of the human, moral essence in all Soldiers, its force in the strength of their personal character and resilience, both on the battlefield and thereafter, is not questioned.[41] As one noted researcher in this field recently concluded, "Religion is a tremendous source of strength, inspiration, wisdom, peace, and purpose for many people and religious speech is a vital component of the practice of religion."[42]

V. RECOMMENDATIONS

Our recommendations are stated here in terse form as we believe they follow logically from the foregoing discussions. They are designed to reinforce the principles in the Army Ethic as discussed in Section II, in particular the understanding that moral leadership is best applied under mission command when the profession's culture is meritocratic and self-policing at each level rather than imposed from above, and when a broad diversity of personal moralities is leveraged to the effectiveness of the profession.

For senior leaders, the Stewards of the Army Profession:

- By policy and personal leadership, maintain the essential meritocratic nature of the Army's Ethic and culture, while celebrating and leveraging the diversity of religious (as well as non-religious) presence within the profession.

- By policy and personal leadership, rid the profession's culture of any real or perceived hostility or intimidation towards religion and its correct expression. Maintain a culture in which Soldiers and their leaders can live and serve with individual authenticity consistent with "military necessity" as expressed in Army regulations. In most all cases, they should be free to express and apply their religious faith and the moral convictions that spring from that faith.

For Soldiers of religious faith, all ranks, uniformed and civilian:

- Be knowledgeable of, and scrupulously follow, your rights to religious expression as well as the limitations to those rights. We recommend a remarkably helpful article by retired Army Judge Advocate General (JAG) officer and current faculty member at the Air Force Academy David Fitzkee, "Religious Speech in the Military: Freedoms and Limitations."[43]

- At the same time, do not overstep your bounds. While serving as integrated leaders of character, and including your moral understanding in all discretionary decisionmaking, remember that you are not called by the Republic in your role as military leader either to be an evangelist for your faith, or to insert your religiously based morality into situations where doing so is improper. So, effectively integrate your personal morality of faith with the profession's ethic: be an integral, authentic leader of character; model the same and develop the same in your subordinates. You have no call to hide your faith or to ignore it in decisionmaking; but your professional call is to **integrate** your faith-based world view and morality with the Army's Ethic, not to redefine the latter.
- Do not be intimidated in the current culture; do not allow the Army's Ethic and culture to be eroded. Get off the sidelines and get engaged. Challenge through official channels all policies/attempts that are hostile to the freedoms of thought, belief, conscience, and correct expression of those convictions, whether based on religion or not.
- Lead up: Expect, remind, and assist the Stewards of the Profession to be the Guardians of the Ethic and the profession's military effectiveness.

ENDNOTES

1. Todd Starnes, "Exclusive: Army halts training program that labeled Christians as extremists," *Fox News*, October 24, 2013,

available from *www.foxnews.com/opinion/2013/10/24/exclusive-army-halts-training-program-that-labeled-christians-as-extremists/*.

2. *Ibid.*, p. 2.

3. Dena Sher and Gabriel Rottman, "Army Right to Halt 'Extremist' Training," *Defense One*, available from *www.defenseone.com/ideas/2013/11/army-right-halt-extremism-training-protect-first-amendment-rights/74102/#.Uouj2OK52HY.twitter?oref=d-interstitial-continue?oref=d-interstitial-continue*.

4. Patrick J. Sweeney, Sean T. Hannah, and Don M. Snider, "The Domain of the Human Spirit," Chap. 2, Don M. Snider and Lloyd J. Mathews, eds., *Forging the Warrior's Character: Moral Precepts from the Cadet Prayer*, New York: McGraw Hill, 2008, pp. 28-29.

5 *Army Doctrine Publication (ADP) 6-22, Army Leadership*, Washington, DC: HQ, Department of the Army, p. 6, paras. 5 and 6.

6. The term "soldiers" will be used to refer to all members of America's military professions, regardless of Service or rank, uniformed or civilian. Later in the monogaph, a capitalized "Soldiers" will be used to refer to all members of the Army, uniformed or civilian.

7. *Department of Defense Instruction (DODI) 1300.17*, Washington, DC: DoD, available from *www.dtic.mil/whs/directives/corres/pdf/130017p.pdf*.

8. *Army Regulation (AR) 600-20*, Washington, DC: Department of the Army, available from *www.apd.army.mil/pdffiles/r600_20.pdf*.

9. See, Robert Audi, "Liberal Democracy and the Place of Religion in Politics," Robert Audi and Nicholas Wolterstorff, eds., *Religion in the Public Square*, Lanham, MD: Rowan and Littlefield, 1997; as well as his more recent book, *Religious Commitment and Secular Reason*, Cambridge, UK: Cambridge University Press, 2000.

10. Christopher J. Eberle and Rick Rubel, "Religious Conviction in the Profession of Arms," *Journal of Military Ethics*, Vol. 11, No. 3, pp. 171-180, quotation from p. 179.

11. See Forum on Religion and Public Life, *"Nones" on the Rise: One-in-five Adults Have No Religious Affiliation*, Washington, DC: Pew Research Center, October 9, 2012, available from *www.pewforum.org*; and Charles Murray, *Coming Apart: the State of White America 1960-2000*, New York: Crown Publishing, 2012, particularly Chap. 11.

12. See Family Research Council, "A Clear and Present Danger: The Threat to Religious Liberty in the Military," Washington, DC (undated report), available from *www.frc.org*.

13. Norton A. Schwartz, "Maintaining Government Neutrality Regarding Religion," memo published on September 1, 2011, available from *msnbcmedia.msn.com/i/MSNBC/Sections/NEWS/z_Personal/Huus/gen_schwartz_letter_religion_neutralilty%5B1%5D.pdf*; and Markeshia Ricks, "Schwartz: Don't Endorse Religious Programs," *Air Force Times*, September 16, 2011, available from *www.airforcetimes.com/article/20110916/NEWS/109160334/Schwartz-Don-t-endorse-religious-programs*.

14. Chief of Staff C. W. Callahan, Commander, Walter Reed National Military Medical Center, "Subject: Wounded, Ill, and Injured Partners in Care Guidelines," Policy Memo 10-015, September 14, 2011, p. 4; "Whoops! Walter Reed Temporarily Bans Bibles," *NBC Washington News*, December 19, 2010, available from *www.nbcwashington.com/news/local/Whoops-Walter-Reed-Temporarily-Bans-Bibles-135853463.html*; and Liz Farmer, "Walter Reed Accidentally Bans Bibles," *Washington Examiner,* December 18, 2011, available from *washingtonexaminer.com/article/151247*.

15. See John Brinsfield and Peter A. Batkis, "The Human, Spiritual, and Ethical Dimensions of Leadership in Preparation for Combat," Chap. 21, Don M. Snider and Lloyd J. Matthews, eds., *The Future of the Army Profession*, 2d Ed., New York: McGraw Hill, 2005, pp. 463-490.

16. Todd Starnes, "Pentagon: Religious Proselytizing is Not Permitted," Fox News Radio, April 30, 2013, available from *radio.*

foxnews.com/toddstarnes/top-stories/pentagon-religious-proselytizing-is-not-permitted.html.

17. Ken Klukowski, "Amendments Protecting Soldiers' Religious Rights Approved by Committee," *Breitbart*, June 7, 2013, available from *www.breitbart.com/Big-Peace/2013/06/07/Congressional-Committee-Protects-Religious-Rights-of-Military-Members*; and, Rep. John Fleming and Senator Mike Lee Press Release, "Fleming Applauds Passage of Religious Liberty Amendment in Senate Committee," June 17, 2013, available from *fleming.house.gov/news/documentsingle.aspx?DocumentID=339355.*

18. Ken Klukowski, "Breaking: Obama Threatens Veto of Religious Protection for Military," *Breitbart*, June 12, 2013, available from *www.breitbart.com/Big-Government/2013/06/12/Breaking-Obama-Threatens-Veto-of-Religious-Protection-for-Military*; and, Office of Management and Budget, Executive Office of the President, "Statement of Administration Policy: H.R. 1960 — National Defense Authorization Act for FY 2014," Washington, DC: The White House, June 11, 2013, available from *www.whitehouse.gov/sites/default/files/omb/legislative/sap/113/saphr1960r_20130611.pdf.*

19. *Army Doctrine Reference Publication* (ADRP) *No. 1, "The Army Profession,"* Washington, DC: Headquarters, Department of the Army.

20. *Ibid.,* pp. 2-3.

21. Peter L. Jennings and Sean T. Hannah, "The Moralities of Obligation and Aspiration: Towards a Concept of Exemplary Military Ethics and Leadership," *Military Psychology*, Vol. 23, No. 5, 2011.

22. See ADP 6-22.

23. *Ibid.,* p. 6, paras. 26 and 27.

24. See Patrick J. Sweeney and Sean T. Hannah, "High-Impact Military Leadership: The Positive Effects of Authentic Moral Leadership on Followers," Chap. 5 in Snider and Mathews, *Forging the Warrior's Character*, pp. 91-116.

25. ADRP1, p. 6-2, para. 6-8.

26. See Paul T. Berghaus, and Nathan L. Cartegena, "Developing Good Soldiers: The Problem of Fragmentation in the Army," *Journal of Military Ethics,* Vol. 12, No. 4 (forthcoming); and, Paul T. Berghaus, "Developing Virtuous Soldiers: Mitigating the Problem of Fragmentation in the Army," M.A. thesis submitted to the Office of Graduate Studies of Texas A&M University, August 2013.

27. *Army Regulation* (AR) *165-1, Army Chaplain Corps Activities*, Washington, DC: Headquarters, Department of the Army, December 3, 2009, available from *www.chapnet.army.mil/pdf/165-1.pdf*; and Todd Starnes, "Army Removes Crosses, Steeple from Chapel," Fox News Radio, January 24, 2013, available from *radio.foxnews.com/toddstarnes/top-stories/army-removes-crosses-steeple-from-chapel.html.*

28. Lieutenant Colonels Peter Fromm, Douglas Pryor, and Kevin Cutright, "The Myths We Soldiers Tell Ourselves," *Military Review,* September-October 2013, pp. 57-68.

29. *Army Regulation* (AR) 15-6 procedures generally govern investigations requiring detailed fact gathering and analysis and recommendations based on those facts. An "investigation" is simply the process of collecting information for the command, so that the command can make an informed decision. AR 15-6 sets forth procedures for both informal and formal investigations. Informal investigations usually have a single investigating officer who conducts interviews and collects evidence. In contrast, formal investigations normally involve due process hearings for a designated respondent before a board of several officers.

Definition available from *www.jrtc-polk.army.mil/SJA/Documents/15-6_IO_%20Guide.pdf.*

30. Authors' discussion with an anonymous Army Officer, September 2013.

31. See Mary Tillman and Narda Zacchino, *Boots on the Ground by Dusk: My Tribute to Pat Tillman,* New York: Rodale Books, 2008.

32. From the Judeo-Christian tradition, consider the 9th Commandment, and the Levitical basis of the West Point Honor Code [Lev. 19:11].

33. The Honorable Charles Johnson and General Carter F. Ham, "Report of the Comprehensive Review of the Issues Associated with the Repeal of 'Don't Ask, Don't Tell'," Executive Summary, Washington, DC: Department of Defense, November 30, 2010, p. 2, available from *www.defense.gov/home/features/2010/0610_dadt/DADTReport_FINAL_20101130(secure-hires).pdf.*

34. *Ibid.*, pp. 11-12.

35. *Ibid.*

36. *Ibid.*, p 13.

37. We say "official," meaning those policies of an ethical nature adopted by the Congress and the Executive under constitutional based processes, such as the repeal of DADT.

38. ADRP1, p. 2-2, para 2-8; and p. 6-2, paras. 6-5 to 6-8.

39. *Ibid.*, Chap. 2, "Trust—The Bedrock of our Profession"; and James Burk, "Expertise, Jurisdiction, and Legitimacy of the Military Profession," Chap. 2 in Snider and Mathews, *The Future of the Army Profession,* pp. 39-60.

40. Jay Allen Sekulow and Robert W. Ash, "Religious Rights and Military Service," Chap. 6, James E. Parco and David A. Levy, eds., *Attitudes Aren't Free: Thinking Deeply About Diversity in the US Armed Forces,* Montgomery, AL: Air University Press, pp. 99-138.

41. For one such effort, see Patrick J. Sweeney, Jeffrey E. Rhodes, and Bruce Boling, "Spiritual Fitness: A Key Component of Total Force Fitness," *Joint Force Quarterly,* Issue 66, 3rd Quarter, 2012, pp. 35-41.

42. David E. Fitzkee, "Religious Speech in the Military: Freedoms and Limitations," *Parameters,* August 2011, p. 66.

43. *Ibid.*